PERFECTLY IMPERFECT STORIES

Laurence King Publishing

FOREWORD

STOP!

Before you read this book, I have a very, very important message for you. I am a grown-up, an adult, a person who can say "well, 20 years ago..." Grown-ups in general are not the smartest people in the world. We're very easily distracted, wrapped up in ourselves and our lives, relentlessly in pursuit of something we decided—or were told—is Very Important.

If you're an adult, I'm sorry to tell you this about yourself.

If you're a child, you already know this. Growing up sometimes means forgetting the things you have known since you were born, and then trying desperately to remember them.

Kids know that life is not perfect. Grown-ups are always telling you what to do and how to do it; other kids don't want to play the same way you do; and you don't get to eat ice cream for breakfast. You know that when you started walking, you spent most of your time falling down. When you started feeding yourself, most of the food ended up on the floor (your dog thanks you for that). Every time you tried something, you were mostly really bad at it, and that was okay! You'd just try again.

Something happens as we get older—slowly, then suddenly—we don't want to make a mistake, we don't want to be bad at something, we don't want to not know an answer or not know how to do something.

We want to be *perfect*.
Or at least we want to *appear* to be perfect.

Perfect means something different to everyone, but we can all imagine how it would feel: a small fortress from which we can view the world, safe from the criticism of ourselves and others. To my knowledge, nobody on Earth has reached the summit of perfection, but plenty of people have attempted to scramble up that path.

How boring.

Perfection is mostly a mirage, a trick of the eye. It is life viewed through a very narrow scope, cropping out the truth. The truth is that life does not want to be perfect, life wants to be lived. Life wants you to raise your hand and lift your voice, and for you to look a little goofy in the process. Life is not just a highlight reel of your happiest moments, but the sum total of all your experiences. You are not just your Big Wins but also your greatest sorrows, mistakes, lows, shocks, and surprises. And so is everyone else.

Remember when you close this book that every person you admire or envy, every person you look down on or judge has their own story. That what it looks like on the outside is not always how it feels on the inside. Whatever you are right now is not what you will always be, and the pain that you think sets you apart from the world is what makes you a part of this world.

If you can live a life where you mess up and start over, where you swing and miss, a life with highs *and* lows, great joy *and* great sorrow? *Well, that's just perfect.*

Xo
Nora McInerny

Nora McInerny is an author, social entrepreneur, and podcaster who shares stories about dealing with grief, loss, and difficult times with her characteristic strength and humor, helping others feel less alone. To find out more, please visit noraborealis.com.

CONTENTS

FRIDA KAHLO

"I never paint dreams or nightmares. I paint my own reality."

When Frida Kahlo felt unhappy, she loved nothing more than to pick up her paintbrush and create beautiful and detailed oil paintings in all kinds of bold colors.

Growing up in Mexico, she didn't have an easy start to life. When she was a young girl, she became very ill with a disease called polio that left her right leg thinner than her left, and made it difficult to walk. She worried about what other children would think about her appearance and struggled to feel happy with how she looked.

Frida struggled to feel happy with how she looked

Despite her insecurities, Frida managed to exercise a strong sense of individuality and unconformity throughout her life, refusing to shave her armpits, bushy unibrow, or mustache. Instead, she put all of her thoughts into her colorful clothes, elaborate accessories, and the fresh flowers she wore in her hair—all of which she often painted into her magnificent self-portraits.

When Frida was 18, another terrible thing happened to her: she was involved in a traffic accident that left her badly injured. Courageous Frida had once dreamed of studying medicine and becoming a doctor, but after the accident, the pain was so tremendous that she had spent months at a time lying in bed. It was during this time that she discovered painting pictures as a way to pass the time in her room; think of how boring it must have been in a time before TVs or iPads!

To her amazement, Frida found that she could take all of the bad things that had happened to her—all the unhappiness and sorrow they brought—and create beautiful pieces of art with them.

Through the rest of her life, Frida faced many other hardships, including 35 different operations and a heartbreaking marriage, which led to minor and major depressive episodes that left her tearful and withdrawn. Even so, she always channeled her pain into her art, creating beautiful and surreal paintings that have made her one of the most celebrated figures in art history today.

She channeled her pain into her beautiful art

Prince HARRY

With the Queen as his grandma, Prince Harry didn't have what you'd call an ordinary upbringing.

As a boy, he was third in line to the British throne, but even so, the little boy with ginger hair and a mischievous smile still loved lots of normal things, like pop music, rugby, and his lop-eared rabbit.

When Harry was 12, his mother, Princess Diana, died suddenly in a car accident. Her death was a shock to everyone who knew her.

Grief can affect you in lots of different ways; some people find it hard not to get upset all of the time, but Harry was the opposite. He felt like the best thing to do was to bottle up his feelings, as thinking about his mom would only make him sad and wouldn't bring her back. Even though he always seemed happy when people saw him out and about, behind closed doors, he felt like his life was in total chaos.

Harry bottled up his feelings, seeming happy to the outside world

After 20 years of shutting the world out, he finally opened up about his feelings to a therapist. Harry suddenly realized that he'd been hiding so many overwhelming thoughts that he hadn't dealt with. By talking about how much he missed his mom, he felt a huge weight lift off his shoulders.

Acknowledging his mental health issues made it easier for Harry to keep doing his job, which takes him all around the globe meeting different people. He also created a mental health charity with his brother and sister-in-law called *Heads Together*, which spreads the wonderful message that talking about your feelings can help you to move forward.

He created a charity with his brother and sister-in-law, empowering others to talk about their feelings

Sometimes it can be difficult to have sad thoughts, but like Prince Harry, it can help you to understand what other people are going through and allow you to make a big impact on their lives.

Even though he still misses his mother, Prince Harry's story does end on a happy note. He found his dream princess and married her at a big church ceremony with his family around him, and they lived happily ever after.

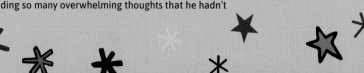

SERENA WILLIAMS

"What matters most is that I like myself."

Serena Williams was just three years old when she started training to become a tennis star. As a little girl, her father would take her to the local court in their hometown of Compton in California, where she'd play for hours in the sunshine against her older sister Venus.

With a powerful serve, lightning-fast reactions, and oodles of energy, the Williams sisters quickly captured the attention of the tennis world, and Serena and Venus became a sporting force to be reckoned with. Serena rose to become the number one tennis player in the world, winning ten Grand Slams and an amazing four Olympic gold medals.

Her incredible power and athletic ability gave Serena the winning edge over her competitors, but over the years, some people have scrutinized her strong and muscular body type. "I always say, 'Not everyone's going to like the way I look,'" says Serena, who has always spoken out against her critics.

"Everyone has different types. If we all liked the same thing, it would make the world a really boring place! What matters most is that I like myself."

A few years ago, when she became a mom, she also battled with something called "postnatal depression," a type of mental health issue that many parents experience after having a baby. It can cause a new mom to feel tearful or anxious, making it difficult for her to bond with her new baby. Serena said feeling sad caused her to worry that she wasn't a good mom.

"I like communication best. Talking things through... lets me know that my feelings are totally normal"

Thanks to a supportive group of family and friends she was able to speak openly about her struggles. "I like communication best," she says. "Talking things through with my mom, my sisters, my friends, lets me know that my feelings are totally normal." Even though she went through tough times off the court, Serena has managed to overcome her mental health problems and return to her sporting career. And to this day, she's still at the top of her game.

DWAYNE JOHNSON

"Have faith that on the other side of your pain is something good."

With his broad shoulders, bulging biceps, and superhero strength, The Rock seems like the type of person that could never be defeated—least of all by something as tiny as a single thought—but that's the funny thing about bad feelings: they can happen to anyone, whether they're tall or short, big or small, confident or shy.

The Rock, of course, isn't his real name. He was born Dwayne Johnson in a city called Hayward in California, and he came from a long line of fearsome wrestlers. As a young boy, he'd play fight with his friends and dreamed of following in the footsteps of both his father and grandfather by becoming a pro wrestler when he grew up.

He reached a point where he didn't want to do anything or go anywhere

His family didn't have much money and when The Rock was 15, their home was taken away from them. Because of the strain, his mother wanted to take her own life and Dwayne's world fell apart. Although he tried to bottle up his emotions, eventually they caught up with him. He reached a point where he didn't want to do anything or go anywhere, and he was constantly crying.

It didn't happen overnight, but The Rock defeated his depression by talking to others. He found the most helpful thing was not to be afraid to open up to other people.

He also threw all of his energy into his dreams of becoming a wrestler. With his dad by his side, he trained to become one of the best wrestlers in the world. By finding his inner strength, he discovered that he was brave enough to follow his dreams, and he was able to help look after his mother, too. The Rock was a natural entertainer. Every time he'd enter the ring the crowds would scream and cheer, but nobody knew that his childhood had been so hard.

He might look big and tough, but sometimes it's easy to forget that even the strongest and bravest people could be struggling underneath the surface.

He found the most helpful thing was no to be afraid to open up to other people

LADY GAGA

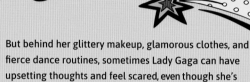

"We are equal. We both walk our two feet on the same earth.

And we're in this together."

Many years ago, there was a little girl called Stefanie who lived in New York, one of the biggest, busiest cities in the world.

Stefanie dreamed of being an international pop star, so she spent all of her time writing songs and singing them to herself in her room—she even learned to play the piano by the time she was just four years old!

Behind her glittery makeup and fierce routines, Lady Gaga can sometimes feel scared and anxious

When she was a teenager, Stefanie went to a special school for singing and acting, and she was so good that her teachers gave her all of the leading roles in her school plays. As she grew up, she started calling herself "Lady Gaga" and when a record company helped her to release an album, her songs went straight to number one and were played all around the world. Now she is one of the most famous singers on the planet with millions of adoring fans who call themselves her "Little Monsters."

But behind her glittery makeup, glamorous clothes, and fierce dance routines, sometimes Lady Gaga can have upsetting thoughts and feel scared, even though she's really confident when she's on stage.

This is because she suffers with "PTSD"—post traumatic stress disorder—which causes people to feel anxious and scared when they're reminded of a frightening moment that happened to them in the past. If you have it, you can experience flashbacks, have horrible nightmares, or find it hard to talk about your feelings. Lady Gaga says her PTSD was caused by a bad event that happened when she was a teenager at school. Even though years and years have passed, she still sometimes has upsetting thoughts that remind her of that time.

She tells herself, "You are brave, you are courageous

Although she can often feel scared if a stranger touches her when she isn't expecting it, it's never stopped Lady Gaga from writing songs, acting in films, or performing in front of huge audiences. She's even won an Oscar!

When she's feeling sad or worried, Stefanie—the girl from New York with a dream to one day be famous—tells herself: "You are brave, you are courageous."

CHARLES DARWIN

"Thus, from the war of nature, from famine and death, the most exalted object which we are capable of conceiving... directly follows.

There is grandeur in this view of life.

In 1831, a young man named Charles Darwin boarded a ship called HMS *Beagle* and sailed out on a death-defying adventure around the world to collect plant and animal specimens.

Although the five-year voyage took him to places as far flung as Sydney and Cape Town, it was in the tropical Galapagos Islands, a beautiful archipelago off the coast of Ecuador, that he made a remarkable discovery.

Darwin watched flocks of small birds called finches flitting around each of the islands, hunting for food. He noticed that each of the creatures had a different type of beak depending on where they lived.

Darwin secretly suffered severe bouts of panic

Darwin's curious mind figured out that all living things are competing to survive, and that those with the most helpful traits for their environment—like finches with small, thin beaks for pecking out nuts and seeds—tend to survive best. These living things then pass along their helpful traits to their young, which explains why plants and animals change over time.

Although Darwin was brave enough to journey to the ends of the earth for his work, he is said to have secretly suffered severe bouts of panic when he felt he couldn't breathe. His heart would race really fast and the feelings could become so upsetting that he felt like he might die, and couldn't help but cry or feel sick.

Darwin also suffered with something called "agoraphobia," which meant that he felt afraid of being out in the open. Sometimes this could trigger a panic attack, but planting his feet on the sands of a new shore always made overcoming his fears worth it.

When Darwin first published his findings from his trip, they were extremely controversial, but today, his "theory of evolution" is thought to be one of the most significant scientific discoveries ever made. You can visit a huge statue of him in the British Museum in London and his face is even printed on the English £10 note.

RUBY ROSE

"I chose to fight and I thought it meant I'd be able to live. I didn't think it meant I'd be able to live my dream."

If you have depression, you never need to feel alone. Approximately 350 million people worldwide have it too, making it a really common illness. It can affect anyone, whether you're a celebrity or not, and treatment—like therapy or medication—is often the most successful way to tackle it.

When she was in her early twenties, actress Ruby Rose, who stars in *Pitch Perfect* and *Orange is the New Black*, took to social media to post a worrying message to her fans, telling them that she was losing her battle with depression.

Ruby was struggling to feel happy when she woke up in the morning and felt like she was failing at being a normal human being

Ruby was struggling to feel happy when she woke up in the morning and felt like she was failing at being a normal human being. Worried but determined not to let it beat her, she canceled everything in her diary, packed her things, and abruptly left her home country of Australia for the US. While in America, she spent all of her money on therapy and going to rehabilitation—a type of program that helps people to get back on their feet.

Ruby was bullied as a teenager and she struggled with bipolar disorder and depression for years. She was 12 when she came out as a lesbian to her mother, which she found hard because she didn't know anyone else who was gay growing up. Feeling uncomfortable with her body, she also thought about changing genders, but now she's older she has realized that she isn't trans—she just didn't identify with traditional stereotypes of women.

Ruby says she's proud that she chose to fight against her depression and it meant she was able to live her dream of being an actress and a role model for young people who identify as LGBTQ+.

Ruby says she proud that she chose to fight against her depression

Reflecting back on that dark time, Ruby wonders how many other people are days, hours, or seconds away from realizing their worth. After successful treatment, her career has gone from strength to strength and she hopes she can inspire others who are struggling to speak out.

EDVARD MUNCH

"For as long as I can remember I have suffered from a deep feeling of anxiety which I have tried to express in my art."

When you pick up your pencils to draw a picture, you might think of scribbling a row of flowers, or a rainbow, or perhaps even a sunny day, but there was one little boy whose drawings were always as dark as night. The faces he drew were unhappy, the colors he used were gloomy, and even swirling strokes from his paintbrush seemed troubled.

This young boy was called Edvard Munch and he lived in Norway. Sadly, he didn't have a very happy childhood. When he was very young his mom and sister died of an illness called tuberculosis. His father lived with depression and his other sister was diagnosed with "schizophrenia"— a condition of the brain that can cause people to see and hear things that aren't real.

Edvard was terrified of becoming sick

Edvard's experiences left him feeling anxious about his own health. He left home to follow his dream of becoming an artist and studied at a special art school in the city of Kristiana, which we now call Oslo. He began to live a very bohemian life—he was extremely poor and spent his days painting and learning from other artists. It was here that he discovered the idea of "soul painting," where you paint your thoughts and feelings.

The most amazing thing about Edvard's mind was that he was always able to turn his struggles with anxiety and sadness into art. Instead of bottling up his feelings, he let his creativity burst onto the canvas in moody colors and sorrowful facial expressions. On his darkest days, he made amazing artworks that people now travel thousands of miles to view in some of the world's most famous art galleries.

He was able to turn his struggles with anxiety and sadness into ar

He painted quite a few famous pictures in his lifetime, but his most iconic was *The Scream*, which is known as one of the art world's most haunting faces. It shows a person screaming on a bridge as two figures walk away into a sunset. Edvard is now studied in schools and universities across the globe as one of the leading figures in expressionism, a type of art movement in which artists try to paint emotion rather than reality—whether that's anger, peacefulness, or, in the case of Edvard, sadness.

WILLOW SMITH

"I honestly felt like I was experiencing so much emotional pain but my physical circumstances weren't reflecting that."

When you grow up, you might dream of being a famous singer, or a TV star in the next big Netflix series. Or maybe you'd like to be a YouTube influencer?

The idea of having millions of adoring fans and lots of money to spend on whatever you want sounds pretty amazing, but it's easy to forget that being famous can have a downside, too.

Willow Smith was only nine years old when she burst onto the music scene with her seriously catchy hit song *Whip My Hair*. Dancing on camera while swinging her braids back and forth, you'd never be able to guess that she hadn't even turned ten yet—she had all the sass and attitude of singers three times her age.

Thanks to its addictive chorus, the song reached number two in the charts and people across the world were hearing it on the radio all the time. Suddenly, little Willow was being asked to go on to talk shows, fans were approaching her for autographs, and the whole world seemed to know her name.

The whole world seemed to know her name

People already knew a bit about Willow, because her parents are pretty famous—her dad is Will Smith, a Hollywood actor, and her mom is comedian Jada Pinkett Smith. But Willow struggled with the sudden attention and found it difficult to handle.

In a conversation with her mom, many years after the song came out, Willow revealed that she felt like she'd lost her sanity while she was swept up in the fame bubble. It made her question who she was and she also began self-harming as a way to cope.

Self-harm is when a person intentionally damages or injures their body. It can be scary and confusing, as often they might not understand why they feel like they need to do it. The reasons can vary from person to person, but it's often a reaction to feeling overwhelmed with emotions that are difficult to express, and it doesn't necessarily mean they want to endanger their life.

One in 12 young people are thought to self-harm, and Willow has spoken about how she's just one of many people that have struggled with it. Looking back, she says she never really talked about her mental health issues, because it was a "short, weird point in my life." Taking the pressure of fame away really helped her, and Willow says she didn't self-harm for long. After her tour and the promotion, she didn't want to finish her album. Instead, she pulled back from the music world and focused on getting better.

FRANK SINATRA

*"I would like to be remembered as a man who had a **wonderful time living his life.**"*

A long time ago there was a very special man. He had sparkling blue eyes, wore sharp, stylish suits, and had an amazing voice that sounded like smooth velvet.

His low, soft voice was so unique it filled concert halls all around the world and made him the first ever big global pop star!

He was called Frank Sinatra and he rose to fame in the 1930s. He was considered a "crooner" in his day, which means he sang emotional songs with a jazz band playing alongside him.

It's amazing to think that Frank was born over 100 years ago, in 1915, but the way people felt about him isn't so different to the way we adore singers today. Instead of listening to him on YouTube or Spotify though, people bought his records and played them on a vinyl player. As a teenager, he performed in nightclubs around town and got spotted by a bandleader who helped him to record his voice, which really set his career in motion.

Even though people loved him and called him affectionate nicknames like "Old Blue Eyes" and "The Voice," Frank often struggled with fame and could find himself with low moods, depression, and feeling like he wanted to be on his own when he wasn't on stage. His depression got worse when his fame started to fade. He lost his voice, was dropped by his record label, and had problems with his marriage to the glamorous actress Ava Gardner.

Depression can be a funny thing and often it might not seem to make sense to everyone around you. For instance, when Frank was famous and surrounded by adoring fans, he could feel lonely, but when his stardom took a downturn, he felt even worse.

Even though there were hard times, Frank wouldn't let his depression stand in the way of his dreams. He picked himself back up and managed to have one of the most amazing comebacks in music, winning an Oscar as an actor and releasing a whole new set of songs that won him many more fans.

> **When Frank was famous and surrounded by adoring fans, he could feel lonely**

He also joined a supergroup called the Rat Pack, that was made up of famous actors and singers from Hollywood's Golden Era in the 60s, like Sammy Davis Jr. and Dean Martin. Frank may have lived with depression, but it didn't keep him off the stage or from recording amazing hits that are still played today.

HÉLOÏSE LETISSIER

"Even if I'm really sad I'm always mending already when I decide to write about it."

There once was a girl called Héloïse who didn't feel like she fitted in anywhere. Growing up in France, she found it difficult to make friends because she felt nervous around the other kids and didn't feel like she wanted to look or behave the same as the other girls.

Because she found it hard to make friends in her classroom, she found fictional friends in the huge piles of books she read, and she felt alive when she was reading about fantastical other worlds and playing make-believe.

As she grew older, she went to a theater school to learn how to put on plays. There she met a boy who became her boyfriend and one of the big love stories in her life. But their relationship was complicated. The boy didn't feel like he looked and behaved like other boys and he felt more comfortable being a girl. He broke up with Héloïse and she fell into a deep, dark depression. At the same time, she got expelled from school.

Feeling sadder than ever, she ran away to London. One night, Héloïse stumbled across a basement nightclub in Soho where a group of drag queens were performing. Drag queens are artists, usually men, that dress up like women on stage. Their larger-than-life personalities, colorful costumes, and carefree attitude amazed her. If they could be queens, then she could be one, too.

The queens took Héloïse under their wing and taught her how to be bold and brilliant. She learned how to express her emotions on stage, and most importantly, how to be herself and not to care about what other people think. After years of feeling like a misfit, she finally felt at home.

She learned how to be herself and to care abou what other people think

Héloïse created a stage name, "Christine and the Queens"—later, simply "Chris"—as a tribute to her beloved pals. Creating songs helped her to survive the lowest point in her life. Feeling empowered, she cut all her hair off and wore what she felt most comfortable in—suits, shirts, and tank tops.

She also told people that she was pansexual, which means you're attracted to people for who they are, no matter whether they're a boy or girl or if they identify as another gender. Creating her own version of what it means to be a woman helped her feel stronger, because she allowed herself to feel comfortable in her own skin. Her music was also a massive worldwide success, and Héloïse—the little girl who felt awkward and shy—became an icon for all the boys and girls who don't feel like they fit in.

WINSTON CHURCHILL

"Never give in, never, never, never, never."

Winston Churchill was one of the great leaders of the 20th century. Famous for his electrifying speeches, he led Great Britain to victory over Hitler and Nazi Germany during World War II, and he also played a big role in gaining peace for Europe once the war came to an end, too.

Winston was born in 1874 at Blenheim Palace, a very grand house near the city of Oxford. His parents were both wealthy aristocrats, and his father was Lord Randolph Churchill, an important Conservative politician at the time.

Winston was sent away to boarding school as a child to get a good education, but he didn't enjoy it very much. He often misbehaved in classes and his teachers said that he didn't do very well in tests.

Intelligent and charming, Winston was a popular character

When he was old enough, he joined the military, serving as both a soldier and a war journalist in many different battles. He read all the books he could get his hands on while he was away, and his experience in countries like Cuba, Afghanistan, Egypt, and South Africa inspired him to start a career in politics when he returned home.

Intelligent and charming, Winston was a popular character with the British people, and he was made prime minister during a really difficult time—when the war was in full swing!

Winston was a great public speaker, not because he said every word perfectly, but because he was so passionate about leading Britain to victory. He suffered with quite a severe lisp, which he worked hard to deal with when he was giving speeches, but that never stopped him from inspiring his people with his infectious energy.

He gave many memorable speeches in his time, such as the "Finest Hour" speech and the speech given before the Battle of Britain. His bold and fearless words inspired the nation to stand strong against Hitler, even when they were the last country left fighting.

Winston was fighting a private battle behind closed doors though. His doctor reported that he suffered prolonged fits of depression, calling them his "black dog." His mental health issues meant he often tossed and turned at night, willing sleep to come.

Winston was known for making the best of his situation and often used his episodes of sleeplessness to his advantage by channeling his energy into his work. He published a whopping 43 books during his time as prime minister, and he even went on to win the Nobel Prize in Literature in 1953. Today, he is celebrated as one of the most influential people in British history.

KYLIE MINOGUE

"There are a lot of voices in my head. I guess part of that is our brains, they're problem solvers."

Around one in every five adults in the US suffers from a mental health problem, and anxiety is one of the most common that people come up against. While you might imagine a person that feels worried or afraid to be shy and quiet, it's important to remember that even confident people that can stride on stage and perform in front of huge crowds can be anxious, too.

Take Kylie Minogue, for example. The Australian singer is one of the biggest female pop artists of all time, with a career that spans over 30 years. She originally became famous as an actress in the 1980s when she appeared in the TV program *Neighbours*, but she made the leap to become a singer and has since sold over 80 million records around the world.

She can fill huge stadiums with thousands of screaming fans

She can fill huge stadiums with thousands of screaming fans today, and she's topped the billboards with disco hits like "I Just Can't Get You Outta My Head" and "Spinning Around."

The Queen of England has even given her a special honor for the amazing music that she's created. It's really no wonder that people have given her the nickname, "The Princess of Pop!"

But even now she's in her 50s, Kylie says that she still struggles with anxiety. She describes how the voices in her head can "tick tick" away when she's trying to solve a problem and her thoughts are racing.

When she's feeling this way, Kylie says that simply stepping away from her anxieties by putting the kettle on and making a cup of tea can really help. Her grandma also taught her a special trick years ago: you lie flat and put your arms up in the air behind your head, and then relax in that position for ten minutes.

Whether she's at home or on a busy video shoot, kylie says she alway makes time to switch off

Whether she's at home or on a busy video shoot, Kylie says she always makes time to switch off. She'll turn her phone to silent, dim the lights, and allow herself to be still until the anxiety eventually passes.

MICHAEL PHELPS

"It's OK to not be OK."

American swimmer Michael Phelps is one of the greatest athletes of all time. With his strong arms, long torso, and big feet, he can thrash through the water with amazing speed, power, and strength, leaving his competition in the dust. In fact, at the Olympics in Beijing, some fans even nicknamed him "half man, half fish!"

During his glittering career, he's won a whopping 28 Olympic medals and 23 of them are gold. Yet, despite all those medals and the praise that came with them, the swimmer extraordinaire has struggled with depression and anxiety.

Despite all those medals and the praise that came with them, the swimmer extraordinaire has struggled with depression and anxiety

A few years ago, it became so bad that he locked himself in his bedroom and stayed there for days, barely eating or sleeping. At some points he felt like he didn't want to carry on living.

Michael says that it was always after the Olympic Games ended that he'd crash and experience these lows. After one really bad spell, he decided it was time to go to therapy. On the first day of walking in to treatment, he was so nervous he was shaking, but he knew he had to figure out what was going on.

To his relief, Michael found that talking to someone really helped to manage his stress. In the past, he'd tried to bury any thoughts or feelings that he didn't want to deal with, which only made the situation worse. Dealing with his issues head-on helped him to realize that it's OK not to be OK, and he hopes that sharing his experience with mental health will help others to open up, too.

Michael found that talking to someone really helped to mana his stress

While people might think that athletes are superhumans that don't have any problems, Phelps says that that's the wrong way to think of it, because they're just like everyone else. Now he's thankful that he can ask for help when he needs it.

MARIE CURIE

"Nothing in life is to be feared, it is only to be understood."

Marie Curie was a brilliant scientist. Her research helped us to discover X-rays, which let doctors see images of bones inside someone's body to check if they have any breaks or sprains.

Ever since she was a young girl, Marie had loved science. When she grew up she wanted to learn as much as possible and went to Paris to study. When she was in Paris she met another keen scientist called Pierre, who soon became her husband.

One day when the two were examining the periodic table—a colorful chart that has all the different elements in the world—they made an amazing discovery. They found two completely new elements called polonium and radium.

This was a true scientific breakthrough, which astounded the world and won the pair a Nobel Prize—a type of award that's given to the brightest people who make amazing discoveries that benefit mankind! It was big news at the time because Marie was the first woman to win the prize, and she's still the only woman to ever win it twice (she was awarded a second Nobel Prize ten years later).

Marie Curie was known for her mind-fizzing brilliance, but she didn't have an easy start to life. She was born in Poland in 1867, and when she was just ten years old, her sister passed away from typhus fever. Two years later she also lost her mother to a type of illness called tuberculosis. Marie was very close to her mom, who had taught her how to read and study even though it was forbidden for girls to go to school in Poland at that time.

Losing her mom and sister was very tough for Marie, and she suffered with episodes of depression. She felt sad, withdrawn, and often didn't feel like eating.

Even though these mental health episodes were very tough, Marie didn't let this stop her doing her favorite things like learning and carrying out scientific experiments. In fact, when she felt sad, she used her brilliant mind to focus even harder on her work.

When Marie felt sad, she used her brillia mind to focus even harder on her work

Fearless Marie eventually died from exposure to radiation, aged 66. Using her work, doctors have been able to build on her discoveries to help give hope to millions of cancer patients around the world. Today she is widely recognized as one of the most important and extraordinary scientists in history.

JOHN GREEN

"I want to talk about it, and not feel any embarrassment or shame."

Everyone experiences anxiety at times. For example, it's normal to feel anxious when you're on a rollercoaster, or before a test. But when your anxiety feels overwhelming—and if you haven't found the right coping skills—it can feel like your worries are whizzing around your mind like fireworks.

He kept thinking about things that made him scared or anxious

A few years ago, John Green felt like he couldn't escape the spiral of his own thoughts. He kept thinking about things that made him scared or anxious and it made it impossible for him to concentrate on writing his bestselling books.

If you love to read, you might already have one of his books on your shelf in your bedroom. As an author, John Green has written lots of different books, but his most famous one is called *The Fault in our Stars,* which is a love story about two teenagers who meet while battling cancer. He's sold millions of copies around the world and is also a YouTube vlogging star.

John says that he's suffered with anxiety and OCD for as long as he can remember. OCD—obsessive compulsive disorder—is a type of mental health issue that causes people to have unwanted thoughts, feelings, and fears. You might have to do or say certain things to relieve your fears, and these actions are called compulsions.

John has said that he keeps his anxiety under control with medication and therapy, where you speak to someone about how you feel. He's also used his experiences with his mental health as inspiration for his real and relatable characters. After he went through a particularly bad time with anxiety, he wrote the book *Turtles All the Way Down,* about a sixteen-year-old girl called Aza who has struggles with OCD, which makes her obsessively fear that she's unwell and that something is wrong with her body.

He's also created YouTube videos to explain to people what it's like to have OCD and how he copes with his compulsions, as a way to help others understand what he and millions of other people around the world are going through.

He's also created YouTube videos to explain to people what it's like to have OCD and how he copes with his compulsions

EMMA STONE

> "My mom always says that I was born with my nerves outside of my body. But I'm lucky for the anxiety, because it also makes me high-energy."

The first time Emma Stone had a panic attack, she was sitting in a friend's house and suddenly felt really scared that it was going to burn down. She immediately called her mom in tears and asked her to pick her up, and for the next three years, the feeling would come back again and again.

If you've had a panic attack before, you might know what Emma felt like. It's a sudden rush of fear that can make your heart beat really fast, your hands shake and cause your mind to feel dizzy, like you've just stepped off a ride at a funfair.

It can happen out of the blue, and it's triggered by your body's fight-or-flight response, which is designed to help you run if something dangerous is happening, like if there was a big, scary tiger in the room. Most of the time, when a panic attack happens, there's actually no real danger and there's nothing to be scared of.

Emma went to see a therapist and she created a book in which she drew a picture of a little green monster sitting on her shoulder, resembling her anxiety. She called the picture "I Am Bigger Than my Anxiety." The monster would grow whenever she listened to it and would shrink whenever she didn't.

Things changed when she discovered acting. To her amazement, she found that improv—a type of theater where you think of the lines on the spot—could help her to feel confident and use her anxiety in a productive way. Being a part of her local children's theater also kept her from spending time alone after school.

She found that improv could help her to feel confident and use her anxiety in a productive way

As time went on, the monster got smaller and smaller. Emma says that the world is hard and scary and that worrying about life can make it hard to do normal things. But if you don't let it boss you around, and use it for something productive—it's like a special superpower!

Her acting superpower took her to Los Angeles, where she became a world-famous star on the screen. She's appeared in loads of hit films and she's got a house full of awards, including an Oscar for "Best Actress."

Today, she keeps her mind happy by going to therapy, practicing breathing exercises, and staying off social media. Emma says: "To be a sensitive person who cares a lot, that takes things in a deep way, is part of what makes you amazing and is one of the greatest gifts of life."

EMMA

GISELE BÜNDCHEN

"Everything I've lived through, I would never change, because I think I am who I am because of those experiences."

When she was just 14 years old, Gisele Bündchen was spotted shopping in her local grocery store by a model scout—a person whose job it is to find the next big face who could be on the cover of magazines like *Vogue* and *Elle*.

With her long blonde hair, perfect skin, and beautiful Brazilian looks, the scout knew they had found someone really special. And they were right! By the time she turned 20, Gisele was one of the world's hightest paid models and she was flying all around the world to strut down runways and pose in front of the cameras.

Even though her life seemed very glamorous, Gisele was really busy, which could be quite stressful. She wasn't sleeping well, she was away from home all the time, and she wasn't eating very healthily either. It all became too much for Gisele when she found herself on a bumpy plane ride while traveling from one country to another. Even though turbulence is normal and very common

Gisele couldn't help but panic and feel like she didn't have any control

when you're flying in bad weather conditions, Gisele couldn't help but panic and feel like she didn't have any control.

After that day, she developed "claustrophobia," a type of mental health issue that makes you feel trapped in confined spaces like planes, elevators, and tunnels. As her fears got worse, she soon found it difficult to be in modeling studios, cars, and hotel rooms without panicking—especially if she couldn't open the windows.

Gisele finally went to see a doctor to get help. She began to get lots of sleep, ate healthily, and woke up at 5am to practice yoga. She also meditated, which involves sitting still, clearing your mind, and paying attention to the sounds and sensations that are happening around you. She found that making simple changes to her lifestyle really helped her to stay relaxed. After three months practicing her new daily routine, the panic attacks began to go away. Now she's older, Gisele looks back on her younger years and says that while things can look perfect to everyone else on the outside, you never have any idea what's really going on.

She found that making simple changes to her lifestyle really helped her to stay relaxed

RAFAEL NADAL

> "No one fails if he does his best to win."

Wimbledon champion Rafael Nadal has been playing tennis for as long as he can remember. When he was just three years old, his uncle—who was a former professional tennis player—bought him a racket and taught him how to play in the courts near his home in Majorca, an island off the coast of Spain that's known for its hot weather, beautiful beaches, and turquoise water.

Rafael was a natural at scoring points against his opponents, and he soon began winning competitions as a teenager. It was then that his uncle told him he needed to choose between tennis and playing soccer, a sport he was also brilliant at, if he was going to become a world champion.

He's dedicated himself to being the best in the game, winning 18 Grand Slam singles titles

It was a tough decision, but sporty Rafael chose to become a professional tennis player at the age of 15. Since then, he's dedicated himself to being the best in the game, winning 18 Grand Slam singles titles—the most important competition in the world of tennis—and even an Olympic gold medal. He has also ranked as the number one tennis player in the world.

A few years ago, Rafael experienced a painful back injury that meant he had to undergo a complicated operation to help repair the damage. The injury affected both his training and his performance on the court, which meant his scores started slipping. Devastated Rafael went from being the best in the world to number five, which he found really hard to come to terms with.

Devastated Rafael went from being the best in the world to number five

It's easy to doubt yourself when you're not at your best, and Rafael said that the thoughts that were running through his mind produced an anxiety that he'd never experienced before.

His feelings of worries and unease lasted for around six months, and he says it was all related to the stress of feeling injured. Now that he's recovered and is back on top form, he feels like he's overcome his worries and has thankfully never experienced the same anxiety again.

SAM SMITH

"Thank you for helping me celebrate **my body AS IT IS.**"

Being a pop star might seem glamorous from the outside, but it can often be more stressful than it looks.

Sam Smith was an unknown singer from London when they shot to fame overnight as the voice on the smash hit song "Latch" by electronic musicians Disclosure. Sam became very famous in a very short space of time, topping the charts and even winning an Oscar for the James Bond theme tune, "Writing's on the Wall."

The celebrity lifestyle was a big change and it took Sam years to feel comfortable in the spotlight. Sam says that

The celebrity lifestyle was a big change and it took Sam years to feel comfortable in the spotlight

flying their family around the world to provide support is a huge help.

Sam has also battled with something called "body dysmorphia," a mental health condition where a person is convinced that there are huge flaws in their appearance, but to other people there is nothing wrong with how they look. Now, Sam has decided to fight back against their fears and love their body for what it is, rather than trying to change it.

Telling the world that they identify as "non-binary," rather than male, has been a huge weight off Sam's shoulders, too. "Non-binary" means that your gender blends different elements of being a man or a woman, or you might feel like your gender doesn't fit into either of those categories.

Instead of calling Sam "he" or "him," they prefer that people now use gender-neutral pronouns such as "they" or "them" when they're speaking to them. Now more than ever, Sam says they are embracing themself for who they truly are, inside and out.

Sam has also battled with something called "body dysmorphia"

Now though Sam has decided to fight back against their fears and love their body for what it is

ARIANA GRANDE

"We will not quit or operate in fear."

Staring out at the star-studded crowd at the Billboard Music Awards, Ariana Grande's eyes filled with tears as she thanked all of the people in her life who'd helped her get to this moment.

With her hair tied into her trademark ponytail, her eyes slicked with black eyeliner, and her glamorous purple dress matching her knee-high boots, she looked every bit the pop star as she collected her award for "Woman of the Year." This was the moment she'd been dreaming of her whole life.

As a girl, Ariana loved performing and was always singing and dancing wherever she went. She won all the leads roles in the plays put on by her local theater group in Florida because she was effortlessly able to hit some of the highest notes in the octave, filling the theater with her jaw-droppingly amazing voice.

She got noticed by Broadway when she was 13 years old and was cast in a theater show, but she got her big break on kids' TV, playing the ditzy Cat Valentine in the Nickelodeon show *Victorious*. Even though she proved popular on TV, she really wanted to pursue the dream of a lifetime—to sing on stage! She launched her music career and has since sold millions of records and has even won a Grammy award for her songwriting.

That doesn't mean life has always been easy for Ariana though. She says can have days where everything overwhelms her and she has to take deep breaths to get through it.

After a devastating explosion at one of her concerts, she's talked about how she suffers from "PTSD"—post traumatic stress disorder—a type of anxiety that's caused by a frightening event. If you have PTSD, you might relive the traumatic event through nightmares and flashbacks, and you might have feelings of loneliness, anger, and guilt, too.

Ariana says she felt like she was floating outside of her body for months after that tragic day, feeling like she couldn't breathe properly because of how it had affected her mentally.

The "7 Rings" singer has spoken to a therapist to help her deal with her scary symptoms. She's also talked about them honestly on her Instagram and Twitter accounts too, to help her fans see that it's OK to be vulnerable.

It's OK to be vulnerable

Even the most confident people can struggle with anxiety, and as Ariana proves, you can often turn your vulnerability into something helpful—like beautiful songs that other people can find comfort in.

LUDVIG VAN BEETHOVEN

"There have been thousands of princes and will be thousands more; there is only one Beethoven!"

Beethoven is one of the most recorded and performed musicians of all time, and if you've ever learned an instrument in school or played in an orchestra, there's a good chance you'll have played at least one of his pieces.

He's easily one of the greatest musical geniuses that ever lived

He's easily one of the greatest musical geniuses that ever lived, but his music is all the more amazing because he wrote most of it while he was completely deaf. Imagine playing the piano and not being able to hear the sounds you're making!

At the end of the premiere of his most well-known piece of music, the *Ninth Symphony*, he famously turned around from his piano and realized, to his shock and surprise, that the audience were on their feet clapping and cheering. Beethoven had no idea that the crowd were going wild behind him, because he could barely hear a thing.

Amazingly, Beethoven composed his best works while suffering with quite severe mental health issues. Some people believe that he had "bipolar disorder," a type of condition which can make you feel very low for days or weeks, while other periods you feel incredibly happy and energized, hardly needing to sleep. If you have bipolar, you can swing between these high and low moods with normal periods of time in between, which can make living life normally quite complicated.

Many creative geniuses have suffered with bipolar though, and Beethoven's friends often talked about days where he'd suddenly have lots of energy, ambitious plans, and ideas. When he was feeling really positive he'd have creative bursts where he could compose lots of amazing music in one go.

When he withdrew from the world, Beethoven's love of music was the thing that kept him going

Although he was challenged by depressive episodes, and they weren't easy to deal with, Beethoven created some incredible music in his lifetime. In fact, it was in his low moods that he composed some of his most memorable pieces, as this is when he withdrew from the world and his love of music was the thing that kept him going.

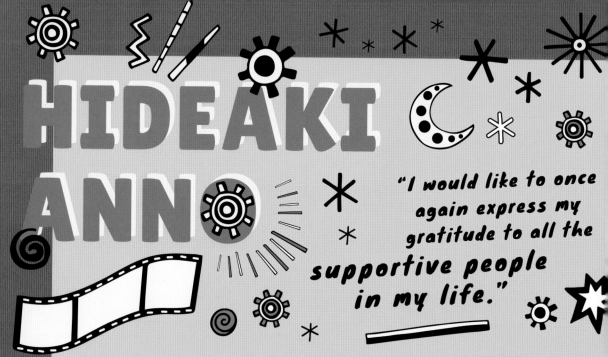

HIDEAKI ANNO

> "I would like to once again express my gratitude to all the supportive people in my life."

Not so long ago, there was a boy called Hideaki who grew up in Japan. Hideaki was super creative and he had a huge imagination, but he didn't get along with school too well. He much preferred to lose himself in the imaginary worlds of manga and anime—types of Japanese films and books.

Hideaki spent his teens making art and short films in his spare time, and although he struggled with focusing on his studies, his special and rare hobby meant that he could find friends outside of school who loved all of the same things as him.

Hideaki would pour his entire heart and soul into each project

Desperate to chase his dreams, he moved to Tokyo to make anime films where he'd animate all kinds of fantasy creatures. Hideaki would pour his entire heart and soul into each project, throwing all of his energy into making every brush stroke look perfect. Even though he put everything he had into these amazing works of art, once each film was finished,

he'd fall into a deep depression that left him feeling sadder than ever.

Hideaki's issues with depression caused him lots of pain and upset, but he found he could also use his dark feelings as inspiration for his characters on screen.

While he was still battling with his mental health, he started to make *Neon Genesis Evangelion*. The show is all about a very sensitive boy called Shinji who, like Hideaki, was abandoned by his father when he was young. He often has to tell himself "I mustn't run away" to give himself bravery in battle, and many people believe that Hideaki based some parts of the character on himself.

Many people believe that Hideaki based parts of the character on himself

The TV series became a massive success with anime fans across the globe, which gave Hideaki a much-needed boost. In fact, there's even a very fast bullet train named after it in Japan!

Although Shinji went through many ups and downs over the years, the TV show ended on a happy note—Shinji, Hideaki's most beloved creation, decided to start loving himself for who he is.

Hideaki Anno

ZAYN MALIK

"Anxiety is nothing to be ashamed of; *it affects millions of people every day.*"

Zayn Malik, a 17-year-old boy from a small English city called Bradford, saw his life change overnight when he auditioned for *The X Factor* and became a part of One Direction, one of the biggest boy bands to ever exist.

Although the boys only came third in the competition, their catchy songs and cheeky personalities made them popular with teenagers all around the world. Suddenly Zayn's life went from going to school in a sleepy city in Northern England to being swarmed by screaming fans and photographers wherever he went.

Zayn toured the world with his bandmates, performing in front of millions of adoring fans, but after five years of being part of One Direction, he decided it was time to create music on his own.

He suddenly found it really hard to perform on stage alone, because of something called performance anxiety

Even though people loved Zayn's new songs, he suddenly found it really hard to perform on stage alone, because of something called "performance anxiety."

Zayn had to pull out of big stadium concerts just hours before performing, because his performance anxiety would turn into panic attacks that made it difficult to breathe.

Zayn has always been really honest with his fans about his struggles with anxiety. After canceling a show, he told them that he'd been working hard on the fears he experiences around major live solo performances—but that sometimes they can get the better of him.

He has also opened up about some difficult times he had back in his One Direction days, too, when he suffered from an eating disorder. He explained that he would go for two or three days straight "without eating anything at all. It got quite serious, although at the time I didn't recognize it for what it was." Now Zayn understands that his fasting wasn't connected to his weight, but to his emotions.

Zayn has always been really honest with his fans about his struggles with anxiety

These days, Zayn says his anxiety is a lot easier to manage, and that's because he's more comfortable with being on stage and knowing who he is as a performer. Now he sees it as a positive thing, rather than something to dread.

FLORENCE NIGHTINGALE

"How very little can be done under the spirit of fear."

Once there was a girl called Florence who was incredibly smart. Her father taught her everything she needed to know about history, philosophy, and literature from a young age, and she was a natural whiz with numbers. She could also read and write French, German, Italian, Greek, and Latin!

In the time that Florence was born, women didn't have the same opportunities as men, and they were expected to get married, have children, and raise a family, rather than become great philosophers or mathematicians.

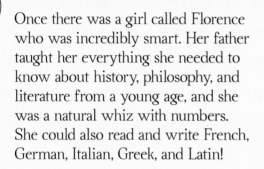

Being kind to others was second-nature to gentle Florence

But Florence was different. She knew that her destiny would take her somewhere important and she felt like she had a calling from God to help other people. Being kind to others was second-nature to gentle Florence, so she decided to train as a nurse. That way, she could spend her life tending to the poor and needy.

Her parents forbade her because they didn't think nursing was a very ladylike job, but she did it anyway, knowing she could make a big difference to the world. During the Crimean War, Florence spent every waking minute caring for the wounded soldiers, who were moved and comforted by her passion for helping strangers. She even got the nickname "The Lady with the Lamp" because she would visit soldiers at all times of the night with a small lantern in her hand. Thanks to her, hundreds of soldiers were nursed back to health, and she helped to make hospitals safer places by using her math skills to record how keeping wards clean and tidy could help sick people get better faster.

Despite her amazing work, some experts believe that Florence Nightingale might have suffered with "bipolar disorder," which can make your moods swing from extremely happy to very sad. Historians who have studied her secret diaries found that she had long periods of feeling down, but her mental health problems were part of her successes, as she also had sudden bursts of productivity—which is why she managed to write over 200 books, pamphlets, and articles on the subject of nursing in her lifetime!

Lots of what we know today about clean hospital conditions is thanks to Florence's hard work and dedication, and even though she struggled with mental health problems, she was still able to save countless lives and change history for the better.

NADIYA HUSSAIN

"I am never ever gonna put boundaries on myself ever again. I'm never gonna say I can't do it."

Each year, a huge white tent appears on the green grounds of a manor house in the English countryside. In this tent, people from all over the UK come to compete in Britain's biggest baking competition, cooking up the most delicious cakes, breads, and pastries you've ever seen.

People fell in love with the superstar baker

It was here, on *The Great British Bake Off*, that Nadiya Hussain captured the hearts of a nation. People fell in love with the superstar baker who made magical creations like a floating cheesecake and giant chocolate peacock. Ever since, she has been one of Britain's favorite bakers, winning lots of awards, presenting her own shows, and writing yummy cookbooks.

But Nadiya almost didn't make it to the competition that would make her famous. She grew up in a busy household with five siblings near London, and as a young girl, she was shy and hardworking but suffered from panic attacks after cruel bullies tormented her at school. Her brother and sister both had life-threatening illnesses as young children, which was hard for Nadiya to deal with. Although life growing up could be hard at times, Nadiya found love and got married at the age of 20. Soon afterward, she decided to learn to bake. She'd spend hours experimenting with mixing together batters and she taught herself everything she needed to know from recipe books and watching videos on YouTube.

Nadiya became busy as a full-time mom to two little boys and a little girl, but behind the scenes, she was still battling with the panic disorder that overwhelmed her at school. Seeing how talented she was at baking, her husband pushed her to apply for *The Great British Bake Off*. He said: "Your wings were clipped somewhere along the way but I think it's time for you to fly."

To her amazement, Nadiya bagged herself a spot on the show. Shy and lacking in self-confidence, Nadiya thought she'd be the one to leave every week—but every week she wowed the judges with her amazing ability to mix together unusual ingredients to make the most incredible flavors. And guess what? She went on to win!

Nadiya has since become one of the most famous and loved British chefs on TV, but she still has days where she doesn't feel 100%. "Some days the monster shouts in my face," she says, but other days, "I can ignore him completely."

KEVIN LOVE

"Everyone is going through something that we can't see."

During the second half of a basketball game against the Atlanta Hawks, Kevin Love stopped hearing noises around him and suddenly felt like he couldn't breathe.

Gasping for air and feeling dizzy, he ran off the court and to the back of the locker room where he collapsed on the floor. He had no idea what was happening—but he knew that whatever it was, it was scary.

Kevin was convinced he was having a heart attack, but after being checked out by a doctor, it turned out that it was actually a panic attack—a sudden onset of fear that can make your heart race really fast, kind of like how you'd imagine a heart attack to feel.

Kevin's teammates were confused about what had happened to make him run out of the game mid-play. Before his on-court panic attack, he'd never really talked about his mental health before.

Boys can often feel pressure to act tough and hide any weakness

Growing up as a young boy in Oregon, Kevin says he learned what he thought it took to "be a man"—which was to be strong and don't ever talk about your feelings.

Boys can often feel pressure to act tough and hide any weakness, especially when it comes to being around their teammates.

Kevin had always been an amazing sportsperson. By the time he turned 16, he was the star player on his high school basketball team and was drafted by the NBA straight out of college.

He's won an Olympic gold medal with the U.S. national team and an NBA Championship with his team the Cleveland Cavaliers.

But at 28, when he suffered a panic attack, he realized that he'd been bottling up his worries for years out of fear that people might think of him as a less reliable teammate. He says he could have really benefited from having someone to speak to.

Kevin says that when you're suffering silently, it can feel like nobody gets you, but looking back, he says he wishes he'd opened up sooner. When he's feeling uncomfortable about his emotions he reminds himself that everyone is going through something that we can't see.

He says he could have really benefited from having someone to speak to

ABRAHAM LINCOLN

"If what I feel were equally distributed to the whole human family, there would not be one cheerful face on the earth."

Over 100 years ago on November 19, 1863, President Abraham Lincoln stood on the Gettysburg hill looking out at a sea of tired but hopeful people, ready to deliver a very special speech.

Just a few months earlier this same place had seen the bloodiest battle of the American Civil War, where lots of people had died while fighting.

The speech was only a few minutes long, but it completely changed the world! We still learn about it in history lessons today, because Abraham talked about how everyone is born equal, at a time when Americans were allowed to keep human slaves to work for them for free.

Abraham talked about how everyone is born equal

As the 16th President of the United States, he's remembered as one of the most influential people in the history of America, but Abraham proves that even great leaders can battle with mental health issues.

He knew great loss and tragedy in his life; he was born in a single-room log cabin in Kentucky, and his father lost everything when his children were young. Abraham's family moved to Indiana and they survived on very little money, plus he had little to no schooling, even though he loved to learn and devoured all the books he could get his hands on. When he was just nine years old, his mother died, and later in his life, he'd go on to lose both of his two young sons.

Depression was a huge part of Abraham's life and he was often struck down by bouts of severe sadness—he would sometimes cry in public and in many of his portraits, he looks gloomy. In fact, an artist working at the White House—the building where the President lives—in the later years of Abraham's life said he had the saddest face that he'd ever painted.

Out of Abraham's sadness came great things though. He's remembered for his amazing speeches and he used his own good and bad experiences to relate to people—so much so they said they could feel his pain when he spoke. He also used coping mechanisms like concentrating on work to help get him through bad spells, and it gave him the strength and courage to handle lots of different crises while he was ruling America.

His passionate work to unite everyone in the country paved the way for the 13th Amendment, which would free all slaves in the United States a few years after he talked about freedom in Gettysburg. Today, people thank and remember him for creating a fairer world for us to live in.

BE KIND TO YOURSELF...

And be kind to others (you never know what someone is going through).

Here are some small steps you can take to support your mental health.

Spend 15 minutes in the sunshine.

Rise and shine. Start each day by making your bed.

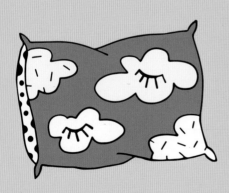

Swim. Take a bath. Move your body in the water and breathe deeply.

Find companionship
in animals.
They make great
listeners.

Express yourself.
Make a piece of art.
Write a poem. Dance...
Move while you are
doing your chores.

Go outside. Spend
time in nature.
Take time to notice
the little things.

keep a journal. Record
the small joys.

Take time out.
Read. Meditate.
Pray. Catch your
breath.

IT'S OK NOT TO BE OK

Need help immediately? Dial 911 for the emergency response line.

If you are in a crisis but don't want to call 911, you can...

- Contact your doctor's office and ask for an emergency appointment.
- Call the Samaritans branch in your area or 1-800-273-8255.

If you are looking for advice or support, here are some organizations that are here to help...

American Academy of Child and Adolescent Psychiatry (AACAP)

A non-profit organization dedicated to facilitating psychiatric care for children and teenagers through advocacy, education, and research. The site contains information about different mental health issues, along with a psychiatrist finder, so you can find support in your area.
202-966-7300 • aacap.org

Child Mind Institute

A charity committed to transforming the lives of children and families struggling with mental health and learning disorders. Their website contains a symptom checker tool and an Ask the Expert page. There is also a wealth of information for concerned caregivers.
childmind.org

Gender Spectrum

A charity that provides useful resources for trans, non-binary, and gender-expansive youths. It also hosts free online group chats to facilitate support and connection.
genderspectrum.org

NAMI: National Alliance on Mental Illness

A grassroots mental health organization dedicated to building better lives for the millions of Americans affected by mental illness, providing support and education for those in need.
1-800-950-6264 • text "NAMI" to 741-741 • nami.org

Teen Line

A confidential teen-to-teen hotline that operates every evening from 6:00pm to 10:00pm PST.
1-800-852-8336 • text "TEEN" to 839-863 • teenlineonline.org

The Trevor Project

A confidential, 24-hour crisis support hotline for LGBTQ+ people under the age of 25.
1-866-488-7386 • text "START" to 678-678 • thetrevorproject.org

Notes

4 "I never paint...reality" : as quoted, Medina, Mariana, *Frida Kahlo: Self-Portrait Artist*, Enslow Publishing 2016; page 129.

6 "Shattering stigma...conversations" : Duke and Duchess of Cambridge and Duke of Sussex, "The Duke and Duchess of Cambridge and Prince Harry lead a nationwide campaign involving several charities to end stigma around mental health." *Heads Together*, April 24 2016. See royal.uk/heads-together-duke-and-duchess-cambridge-and-prince-harrys-campaign-end-stigma-around-mental-health.

8 "I always say...look" : as quoted, Cocozza, Paula, "Serena Williams: 'Not everyone's going to like the way I look.'" The *Guardian*, June 28 2016. See theguardian.com/lifeandstyle/2016/jun/28/serena-williams-interview-beyonce-dancing-too-masculine-too-sexy.

8 "Everyone...like myself" : as quoted, Wilder, Charlotte, "Serena Williams doesn't care if you think she's 'too masculine.'" *USA Today*, June 28 2016. See usatoday.com/2016/06/serena-williams-hits-back-at-critics-too-masculine.

8 "Talking things through...normal" : Serena Williams Instagram post, August 6 2018. See instagram.com/p/BmJ3KMzFRZw/?utm_source=ig_embed&utm_campaign=dlfix.

10 "Have faith...good" : "How a Bout of Depression Led to Dwayne Johnson's Career-Defining Moment." *Oprah's Master Class*, video, 0:38, November 12 2015. See youtube.com/watch?v=y_T9Jg0U2DA.

12 "You are...courageous" : Lady Gaga, "Lady Gaga visits homeless LGBT teenagers." The *Guardian*, video, 0:26, December 6 2016. See theguardian.com/music/video/2016/dec/06/you-are-brave-you-are-courageous-lady-gaga-visits-homeless-lgbt-teenagers-video.

12 "We are equal...together" : as quoted, DiLuna, Amy and Sindler, Robin, "Lady Gaga reveals how kindness has helped her heal while visiting LGBT teens." *Today*, December 5 2016. See today.com/kindness/lady-gaga-reveals-how-kindness-has-helped-her-heal-while-t105575.

14 "Thus...view of life" : Darwin, Charles, *On the Origin of Species*, John Murray, 1859; page 425.

16 "I chose...to live my dream" : as quoted, Saul, Heather, "Ruby Rose 'shook-up' after being reminded of hitting 'rock bottom' with depression." The *Independent*, April 2 2016. See independent.co.uk/news/people/ruby-rose-depression-twitter-orange-is-the-new-black-a6965201.html.

18 "For...my art" : as quoted, Churchill, Tom, "The original emoji: Why The Scream is still an icon for today." *BBC Arts*, April 11 2019. See bbc.co.uk/programmes/articles/32ytpvFgnLxtZNynYJYWbP6/the-original-emoji-why-the-scream-is-still-an-icon-for-today.

20 "I honestly felt...that" ... "short, weird point in my life" : as quoted, Reed, Anika, "Willow Smith reveals to mom Jada Pinkett Smith that she was 'cutting' herself." *USA Today*, May 15 2018. See eu.usatoday.com/story/life/entertainthis/2018/05/15/willow-smith-reveals-she-cutting-herself-after-early-success/610651002/.

22 "I would like...life" : In a 1965 interview with Walter Cronkite, as quoted in "Just A Couple Of Legends," *CBS News*, May 20 1998. See cbsnews.com/news/just-a-couple-of-legends/.

24 "Even if I'm really sad...write about it" : as quoted, Ross, Annabel, "Advice from drag queens turned a depressed queer girl into a global pop star." The *Sydney Morning Herald*, August 31 2018. See smh.com.au/entertainment/advice-from-drag-queens-turned-a-depressed-queer-girl-into-a-global-pop-star-20180827-h14kbf.html.

26 "Never...never" : Churchill, Winston, "A speech given by Winston Churchill, MP at Harrow School," October 29 1941.

26 "black dog" : Moran, Lord, *Winston Churchill: the Struggle for Survival 1940–1965*, Constable, 1966; page 439.

28 "There are a lot of voices...problem solvers" : "Kylie Minogue talks anxiety battle and why 'Golden' is her most personal album yet." *Attitude*, March 29 2018. See attitude.co.uk/article/kylie-minogue-talks-anxiety-battle-and-why-golden-is-her-most-personal-album-yet/17425/.

30 "It's...OK" : Phelps, Michael, "Michael Phelps on managing depression: 'It's OK to not be OK.'" *CBS This Morning*, video, 3:40, September 17 2018. See youtube.com/watch?v=8p3Kdzfb-_c.

32 "Nothing...be understood" : as quoted, Benarde, Melvin A., *Our Precarious Habitat*, W. W. Norton and Company, 1973; page v.

34 "I want...shame" : as quoted, Alter, Alexandra, "John Green Tells a Story of Emotional Pain and Crippling Anxiety. His Own." The *New York Times*, October 10 2017. See nytimes.com/2017/10/10/books/john-green-anxiety-obsessive-compulsive-disorder.html.

36 "My mom...high-energy" ... "To be...gifts of life" : as quoted, Petter, Olivia, "Emma Stone opens up about anxiety and how it gives her 'high-energy.'" The *Independent*, August 16 2018. See independent.co.uk/life-style/emma-stone-anxiety-jennifer-lawrence-elle-interview-a8494161.html.

38 "Everything...those experiences" : as quoted, Triggs, Charlotte, "Gisele Bündchen Says She Battled Panic Attacks So Extreme She Considered Suicide: 'I Felt Powerless.'" *People*, September 26 2018. See people.com/books/gisele-bundchen-panic-attacks-considered-suicide-book/.

40 "No one fails...win" : as quoted, Gatto, Luigi, "Rafael Nadal: 'No one fails if you do your best to win.'" *Tennis World*, December 1 2017. See tennisworldusa.org/tennis/news/Rafael_Nadal/49559/rafael-nadal-no-one-fails-if-you-do-your-best-to-win-/.

42 "Thank you...AS IT IS" : Sam Smith Instagram post, February 12 2019. See instagram.com/p/Btypu_iAaVt/?utm_source=ig_embed&utm_campaign=dlfix.

44 "We will not...operate in fear" : Ariana Grande Twitter post, May 26 2017. See twitter.com/ArianaGrande/status/868164986887176192.

46 "There have been thousands...Beethoven" : as quoted, Beethoven, Ludwig van, Kerst, Friedrich and Krehbiel, Henry Edward, *Beethoven, the Man and the Artist, as Revealed in His Own Words*, Dover, 2016; page 73.

48 "I would like...my life" : as quoted, Baseel, Casey, "Evangelion creator Hideaki Anno opens up about his latest bout with depression, movie delays." *Sora News*, April 2 2015. See soranews24.com/2015/04/02/evangelion-creator-hideaki-anno-opens-up-about-his-latest-bout-with-depression-movie-delays/.

48 "I mustn't run away" : as spoken, Ikari, Shinji, "Angel Attack [1.1]" *Neon Genesis Evangelion*, October 4 1995.

50 "Anxiety...every day" : Malik, Zayn, "Zayn Malik: Why I Went Public With My Anxiety Issues." *Time*, October 31 2016. See time.com/4551320/zayn-malik-anxiety/.

50 "Without eating...what it was" : "Zayn Malik reveals he had eating disorder while in One Direction." *BBC Newsbeat*, November 1 2016. See bbc.co.uk/newsbeat/article/37833903/zayn-malik-reveals-he-had-eating-disorder-while-in-one-direction.

52 "How very little...fear" : as quoted, Cook, John, *The Book of Positive Quotations*, Fairview Press, 1997; page 479.

54 "I am never...can't do it" : Hussain, Nadiya, *The Great British Bake Off* series 6, Episode 10, October 7 2015.

54 "Some days the monster... ignore him completely" : "Nadiya Hussain opens up about her panic disorder 'monster,'" *BBC News*, September 19 2017. See bbc.co.uk/news/entertainment-arts-41318362.

56 "Everyone...we can't see" : as quoted Pawlowski, A., "'Everyone is going through something': NBA star Kevin Love reveals panic attack." *Today*, March 6 2018. See today.com/health/nba-s-kevin-love-reveals-panic-attack-mental-health-struggle-t124554.

56 "Be a man" ... Love, Kevin, "Everyone Is Going Through Something," *The Player's Tribune*, March 6 2018. See theplayerstribune.com/en-us/articles/kevin-love-everyone-is-going-through-something.

58 "If what I feel...earth" : Lincoln, Abraham, "Letter to John T. Stuart," January 23 1841, *Collected Works of Abraham Lincoln*. See https://quod.lib.umich.edu/cgi/t/text/text-idx?c=lincoln;rgn=div1;view=text;idno=lincoln1;node=lincoln1:248.

Published in 2021 by
Laurence King Publishing Ltd
361–373 City Road
London EC1V 1LR
United Kingdom
T + 44 (0)20 7841 6900
enquiries@laurenceking.com
www.laurenceking.com

Text © 2020 Magic Cat Publishing Ltd
Illustrations © 2020 Ana Strumpf
First published in the UK by Magic Cat Publishing

The right of Ana Strumpf to be identified as the illustrator of this work has been asserted by her in accordance with the Copyright, Designs, and Patents Act, 1988.

A catalog record for this book is available from the British Library.

ISBN 978-1-78627-920-0

Published by Rachel Williams and Jenny Broom
Designed by Nicola Price

Manufactured in China, HH0120

Laurence King Publishing is committed to ethical and sustainable production. We are proud participants in The Book Chain Project®
bookchainproject.com

Text by Leo Potion
Foreword by Nora McInerny
Consultancy by Dr. Anna Moore, Clinical Academic in Child Psychiatry, NIHR CLAHRC, University of Cambridge

Photographs © 2020: Alamy stock photo, courtesy: page 5: Lucas Vallecillos; page 7: dpa picture alliance archive; page 9: Adam Stoltman; page 11: AF archive; page 13: Tsuni / USA; page 15: AF Fotografie; page 17: WENN Rights Ltd; page 19: Pictorial Press Ltd; page 21: Allstar Picture Library; page 23: Entertainment Pictures; page 25: Steve Vas; page 27: Everett Collection Historical; page 29: WENN Rights Ltd; page 31: Xinhua; page 33: IanDagnall Computing; page 35: ton koene; page 37: PictureLux / The Hollywood Archive; page 39: Everett Collection Inc; page 41: VICTOR FRAILE; page 43: LMK MEDIA LTD; page 45: LANDMARK MEDIA; page 47: Ewing Galloway; page 49: Aflo Co. Ltd.; page 51: Pictorial Press Ltd; page 53: David Cole; page 55: michael melia; page 57: dpa picture alliance archive; page 59: Ian Dagnall